FOOD AND DIGESTION

Brian R. Ward

Series consultant:
Dr A. R. Maryon-Davis
MB, BChir, MSc, MRCS, MRCP

The Human Body

Franklin Watts
London New York Sydney Toronto

First published in Great Britain 1982 by
Franklin Watts Limited
8 Cork Street
London W1

First published in the United States of America by
Franklin Watts Inc.
730 Fifth Avenue
New York
N.Y.10019

UK ISBN: 0 85166 948 4
US ISBN: 0-531-04458-0
Library of Congress Catalog Card No: 82-50057

Designed by Howard Dyke

Phototypset by Computape (Pickering) Ltd, North Yorkshire
Printed in Great Britain by E. T. Heron, London and Essex

Acknowledgments

The illustrations were prepared by: Andrew Aloof,
Howard Dyke, Hayward Art Group, David Holmes,
David Mallott, Charles Raymond, Ann Winterbotham.

Contents

Introduction

We need to eat to provide energy for the body and building materials for growth and repair.

Food contains a number of essential substances which are normally in a form we cannot immediately use. These substances must be processed and changed in the digestive system so that they can be absorbed into the body. This is the process of digestion.

Oxygen in the air we breathe is used to break down some of these substances further, releasing energy to power all the processes of the body. This energy can also be stored in the form of substances which are easily broken down when needed.

The process of digestion takes place in a long system of tubes running from the mouth to the anus. This is the **gut**, or digestive tract. Within this system, digestion takes place in a series of steps, at each of which different parts of the food are broken down.

Our digestive system is adapted to cope with a very wide range of food material from which we extract the substances we need to grow and remain healthy.

The digestive system consists of a long continuous tube which, together with other organs, helps in the digestion and storage of food.

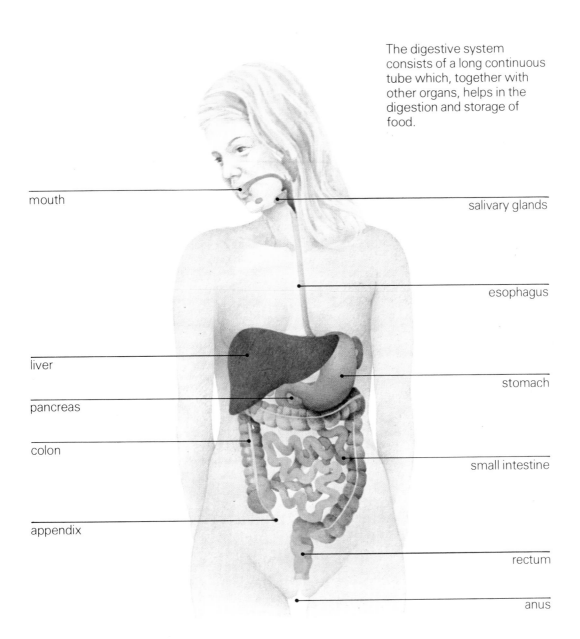

mouth

salivary glands

esophagus

liver

stomach

pancreas

colon

small intestine

appendix

rectum

anus

5

The diet

Our diet consists of a mixture of meat, dairy products, vegetables and cereals. These types of food contain **protein**, **fats**, **carbohydrates**, **minerals** and **fiber** substances in different proportions.

Protein is a very important part of our diet. It is found in large amounts in meat, fish, milk and eggs and in small quantities in vegetable material such as beans, peas, nuts and cereals.

Fats are found in meat, milk and butter. Nuts and a few other vegetable products contain useful quantities of fats.

The main energy source for the body are carbohydrates, which include many different types of **starches** and **sugars**. Foods such as potatoes and bread are rich in starch and sugars. Other sources of carbohydrates include cereals, fruit, sugar and nuts.

A major part of the diet cannot be used at all. This is fiber, consisting mainly of **cellulose**, obtained from vegetable foods. This material is indigestible, and passes out of the body as **feces**, or solid waste. Fiber increases the bulk of the feces, helping it to pass easily through the lower part of the gut.

The final components of the diet are minerals. These materials are mostly needed for growth.

Protein, carbohydrates, fats, minerals, vitamins and fiber are all needed for health, but our bodies can adjust to different levels of each nutrient. The proportion of nutrients in the diet varies widely around the world.

The "Mediterranean" diet is rich in carbohydrates, protein and fats.

The North American and European diets rely greatly on "convenience" foods, which are high in all nutrients except vitamins.

The "African" diet is high in carbohydrates and fiber, but low in protein and fats.

The "Oriental" diet is high in carbohydrate and fiber and includes some protein, but is low in fats.

Using food

Nearly one-fifth of our body weight is made up of protein, and all of this has been obtained from the food we eat. Proteins are made up of very large molecules, too big to pass through the wall of the gut into the body. In the process of digestion protein is broken down into smaller molecules called **amino acids**. These are readily absorbed. Once inside the cells, the amino acids are built up again into protein.

Protein is the chief building material of the body, and our muscles are very largely made up of this substance.

Fats are important as a source of energy, and are present in small amounts in every cell of the body. They also play an essential role in the chemistry of the individual cell. We use fat as an energy store, and it builds up in certain parts of the body. This fat can be broken down to produce energy.

Carbohydrates are quickly broken down to produce energy. They are stored in the liver and other tissues, but are quickly used up during exercise. The body then begins to use its fat, which takes longer to break down.

Minerals are used in large amounts during growth, to build bones, teeth and blood. As adults, we need only small amounts of minerals to replace those lost in the urine.

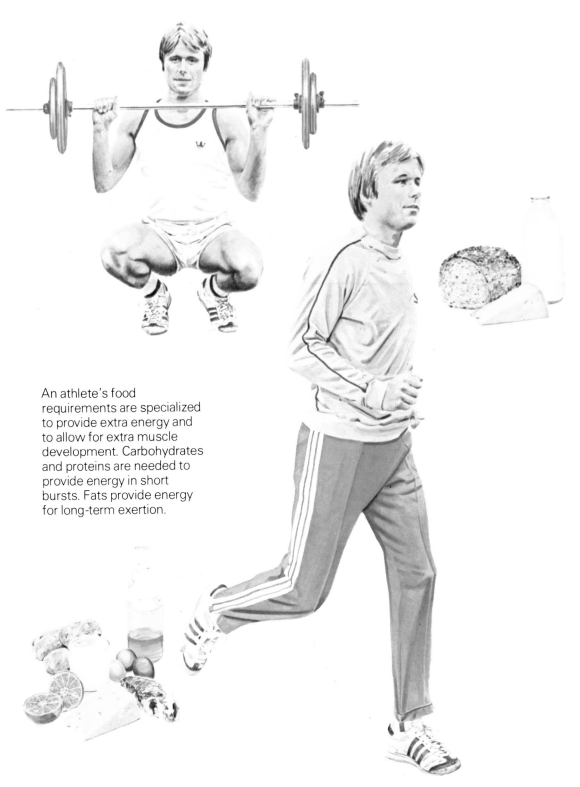

An athlete's food requirements are specialized to provide extra energy and to allow for extra muscle development. Carbohydrates and proteins are needed to provide energy in short bursts. Fats provide energy for long-term exertion.

Vitamins

Proteins, fats, carbohydrates and minerals are all essential for life. But there are many other substances the body must have if we are to remain healthy. These substances are called **vitamins**.

The body needs only tiny amounts of vitamins, and a healthy, balanced diet will include all of these. It is not clear how the body uses most vitamins. What we do know about are the results of vitamin deficiency, when not enough are present. Vitamin C, for example, is present in fresh vegetables and fruit, and it seems to be necessary for cell growth and repair. Vitamin C deficiency can cause the disease known as scurvy, which

Vitamin A
Needed for growth and resistance to infection. It is also important in maintaining healthy skin and eyes.

Vitamin B
Several B Vitamins are important in helping to release energy from food. They are also essential in growth, and in maintaining the health of skin and mucous membranes.

Vitamin C
Necessary to maintain the proper connections between body cells. Helps healing. Vitamin C is not stored in the body and needs constant renewal.

affected sailors on long voyages, when they were without fresh fruit or vegetables.

There are probably 40 or more vitamins, and at least 12 are essential for good health. During our entire lives we use only 3 oz (85 grams) of Vitamin A, and less than 1 oz (28 grams) of thiamine (or Vitamin B_1). Some vitamins can be stored for a while, but others, such as Vitamin C, pass straight out of the body in our urine.

Vitamin D is unusual in that it can be made in the skin, by exposure to sunlight. Even so, millions of children around the world suffer Vitamin D deficiency, which causes the bone-distorting disease rickets.

Vitamin D
Controls the levels of calcium and phosphorus needed for teeth and bones. It is very important in childhood. Vitamin D can be produced in the body by the action of sunlight on the skin.

Vitamin E
Important in reproduction. It influences the chemistry of the growing cell, and helps in wound healing.

Vitamin K
Essential in blood clotting, to stop bleeding from wounds.

The process of digestion

proteins

fats

carbohydrates

amino acids

glycerol

action of enzymes

simple sugars

water

salts

vitamins

absorption and transport to the liver

The main nutrients in our diet are broken down in a series of steps as they pass through the digestive system until they are in a form suitable for absorption. Substances such as water, salts and vitamins need no digestion, and are absorbed unchanged.

Before a food material can be absorbed into the body, it must be broken down into small molecules which are capable of dissolving in water. The process of digestion breaks down complex food molecules that will *not* dissolve into simpler, smaller molecules which can then pass through the wall of the gut. Fat cannot dissolve, but is instead broken down into droplets so tiny that they can enter the cells that line the gut.

Glands along the length of the gut produce acids and **alkalis** which provide the proper conditions for digestion. The most important part in digestion is played by **enzymes**. These are substances, produced in the gut, which help to break down the food. Some enzymes work in acid conditions, while others need alkaline conditions. As the food moves along the gut, it is flooded with mixtures of acid or alkali and enzymes. Together these corrosive liquids break down food substances.

At each stage in its movement along the gut, different substances in the food are broken down and absorbed, until all that remains is waste feces.

The meat we eat is made of the same materials as our own gut, but we do not digest ourselves, due to a protective coating produced by the lining of the gut.

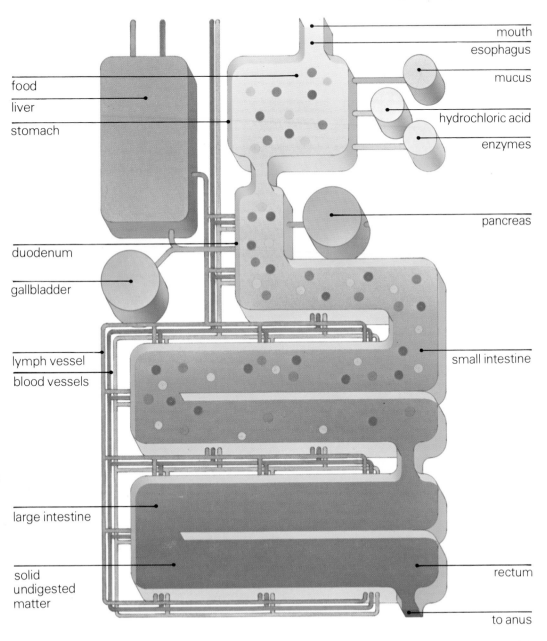

Digestion is a continuous process, with food passing along the tubular gut and being acted on by enzymes and other substances at different points. The diagram shows a simplified version of the digestive system.

mouth

esophagus

mucus

food

liver

hydrochloric acid

stomach

enzymes

pancreas

duodenum

gallbladder

lymph vessel

small intestine

blood vessels

large intestine

solid
undigested
matter

rectum

to anus

The structure of the gut

The gut is a long, continuous tube, starting at the mouth, and ending, about 30 ft (9 m) later, at the **anus**. The gut is a tough tube that remains flattened and collapsed until it contains food or liquid.

A typical section of the gut is made up of several layers of special tissue. The inner layer is called the **mucosa**. This is wrinkled, giving it a large surface area for the absorption of food materials. It also contains many tiny glands which pour out, or secrete, substances such as enzymes into the gut. This layer also protects the gut from its corrosive contents and prevents the bacteria which line the gut from attacking the body.

Next is a layer called the **submucosa**, which is tough and elastic. It contains blood vessels and nerves and also serves to strengthen the gut.

The submucosa is covered by two layers of muscle, one wrapped around the gut, and the other running along in a slight spiral. These two sets of muscle produce the movement called **peristalsis**.

Mucosa. Inner layer, specialized for secretion and for absorption. The layer is mostly folded to increase its surface area.

Submucosa. Tough framework of the tube which contains blood vessels and nerves.

Muscle layers. These work together to produce the churning action of peristalsis.

Outer coating, or serosa. Protects and lubricates the surface of the digestive system. Some parts of the gut are further covered by the mesentery.

Most of the digestive system is constructed to a similar plan, adapted in some areas to allow for special digestive processes. The whole length of the digestive system is a muscular tube made up of several layers.

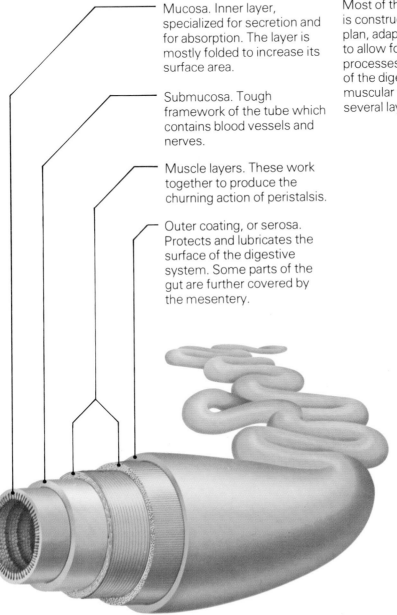

15

Peristalsis

Peristalsis is the muscular process which moves food along the intestine.

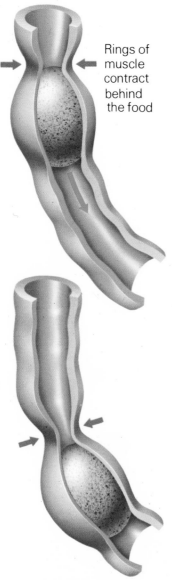

Rings of muscle contract behind the food

The area of contracted muscle moves down the intestine like a wave, pushing the food material before it.

The gut is very long and is packed tightly in the chest and abdomen. Food cannot pass freely along the tubular gut unless it is pushed. The process of peristalsis moves the food along, lubricated by a layer of slippery **mucus**, which is secreted by the mucosa.

Peristalsis is carried out by the two layers of muscle in the gut wall. First, muscle wrapped around the gut shortens, or contracts, squeezing and narrowing the gut just behind the food. Then the muscle which runs along the gut contracts, shortening the length of gut. At the same time the narrowed portion moves down the gut, pushing the food with it. The effect is just like pushing a ball along inside a sock by running the sock through your clenched fist. This peristaltic movement is continuous, like a wave, pushing small lumps of food, one after the other. Peristalsis continues throughout the digestive system, slowing to allow digestion to take place, then speeding up to push the food along to the next stage in digestion.

If the gut is irritated by infection or by substances in the food, peristalsis may be too rapid for proper digestion to take place, causing diarrhea. If it is too slow, or weak, the food is not moved along, and constipation results.

Vomiting is caused when peristalsis works in reverse to eject food from the stomach, aided by violent contraction of the stomach and abdomen wall.

Food passes slowly through the digestive system. It takes 12 hours or more from the time that food enters the mouth until feces are discharged from the anus. The speed of the passage of food is controlled by peristalsis.

Food is chewed and swallowed.

Food takes only seconds to pass down the esophagus to the stomach.

Food remains in the stomach for anything from 5 minutes to several hours.

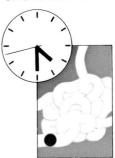

After about 4½ hours partly digested food has passed along the small intestine.

After 5½ hours liquid feces enter the colon. Digestion is now complete.

6½ hours on, and the feces are starting to solidify.

After 9½ hours the feces are almost solid.

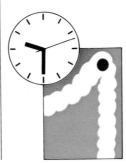

12 hours later. Feces reach the rectum ready for discharge.

The mouth

The mouth is a complicated mechanism for tearing, cutting, and grinding food into conveniently small pieces ready for digestion. It also softens and moistens chewed food.

The lips and tongue are very muscular and position food in the mouth so that it can be broken up by the teeth.

The lower jaw is also very mobile, and can be moved to and fro and from side to side, as well as performing the normal biting movement.

Our teeth are grouped on the upper and lower jaws, in such a way that they can carry out several important tasks. A child has 20 "milk" teeth, which are shed as the 32 adult teeth emerge over a period of several years. The front teeth, the incisors, cut the food in a biting action. Next to them are the sharply pointed canine teeth, used for tearing tough food. At the back of the jaws are broad premolar and molar teeth. These have a series of sharp points and ridges to grind food as we chew.

Digestion actually starts in the mouth. Saliva is poured over the food from glands in the sides of the mouth and below the tongue. Saliva helps to pack the chewed food into a moist pellet ready for swallowing. Saliva also contains **ptyalin**, an enzyme which converts

Salivary glands produce a watery mixture of mucus and the enzyme ptyalin. This lubricates chewed food and begins the digestion of carbohydrates.
Many small salivary glands are dotted throughout the cheeks and palate.

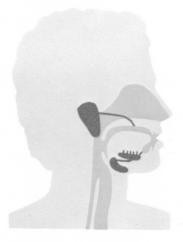

tasteless starch into sugar within the mouth. That is why bread, which contains starch, begins to taste sweet as it is chewed.

Finally, the tongue positions the food at the back of the mouth, where it is swallowed.

The adult jaw contains 32 teeth which are specialized for cutting, tearing and grinding food.

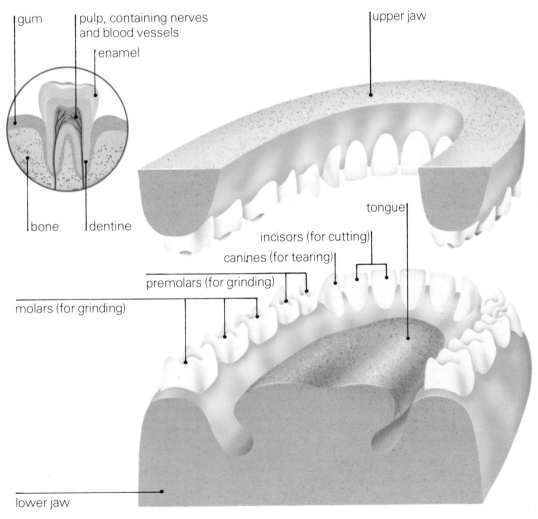

gum

pulp, containing nerves and blood vessels

enamel

bone

dentine

upper jaw

tongue

incisors (for cutting)

canines (for tearing)

premolars (for grinding)

molars (for grinding)

lower jaw

19

The esophagus

Swallowed food passes toward the back of the mouth and then through the pharynx. At the base of the pharynx is a flap called the epiglottis. During swallowing the epiglottis closes off the windpipe so that food does not enter the lungs. Wavelike peristalsis then carries the food down the **esophagus**, or gullet, into the stomach.

The esophagus is a short tube, about 10 in (25 cm) in length, which runs down through the chest. It passes behind the heart, before curving forward to enter the stomach.

The lower end of the esophagus passes through the muscular sheet of the diaphragm, which separates the contents of the chest from the abdomen. Just below the diaphragm the muscles in the esophagus wall are particularly strong and can pinch the tube shut, to prevent food in the stomach from rising back up the esophagus.

Because the esophagus carries chewed, undigested food which may still be rough or sharp, it has a special lining to resist wear and tear. It is also capable of stretching to allow lumps of food to pass along, and has stronger muscles than other parts of the system.

Peristalsis carries food or liquids along the esophagus no matter what the position of the body.

The muscular esophagus pushes food and drink along by peristalsis. It works just as effectively if you stand on your head, or even if there is no gravity, as in a spacecraft.

The stomach

The stomach stores food temporarily, as food passes along the digestive system. At the same time it plays an important part in digestion.

The stomach is a large muscular bag, situated near the bottom of the chest, which can hold up to 3 pints (1.5 liters) of liquid and food. It is shaped rather like a curved pear, pointing downwards and to the right. The

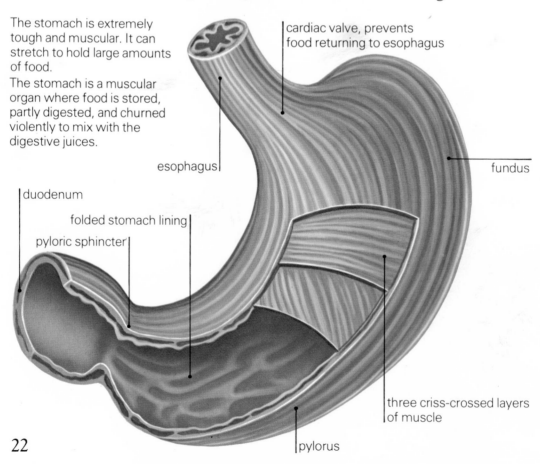

The stomach is extremely tough and muscular. It can stretch to hold large amounts of food.

The stomach is a muscular organ where food is stored, partly digested, and churned violently to mix with the digestive juices.

cardiac valve, prevents food returning to esophagus

esophagus

fundus

duodenum

folded stomach lining

pyloric sphincter

three criss-crossed layers of muscle

pylorus

Food enters the stomach from the esophagus. Food piles up in the upper part, the fundus, where it is stored temporarily, before being gradually passed down to the lower end, or pylorus.

The pylorus churns food vigorously, mixing it with enzymes, acid and mucus.

Partly digested food is continually ejected in small amounts through the pyloric sphincter into the duodenum. More food then passes down from the fundus to undergo the same process.

esophagus enters near the broad top part of the stomach, called the **fundus**.

The lower part of the stomach, called the **pylorus**, is where part of the process of digestion takes place. The pylorus is very muscular and churns the food to aid in digestion.

The stomach usually contains a small amount of gas, as a result of our swallowing air with our food. The presence of this gas allows the liquefied food to slop about as it is churned by peristalsis, causing "stomach rumbling."

A large meal may remain in the stomach for as long as six hours. After this time its contents are pumped out into the next part of the digestive system, the **duodenum** of the small **intestine**. Food leaves the stomach through a circular valve of muscle, called the pyloric **sphincter**. This is similar but much stronger than the valve leading into the stomach from the esophagus.

Digestion in the stomach

The stomach plays an important part in breaking down food materials, but does not absorb digested foods.

The stomach is lined by mucous membrane, containing many millions of tiny gastric glands which produce gastric juice. This contains **hydrochloric acid**, a highly corrosive liquid which causes the sour taste when we vomit.

The gastric glands also produce a substance called **pepsinogen**. When this meets the acid stomach contents, it is converted into the enzyme **pepsin**. At the same time, the hydrochloric acid destroys bacteria present in the food and softens tough food materials. Working in these strongly acid conditions, pepsin begins to break down protein into a usable form.

A baby's stomach produces another enzyme called rennin, which curdles milk, causing it to clot, so that the protein it contains can start to be digested in the stomach. In adults, who no longer produce rennin, milk passes straight to lower parts of the system for digestion.

Another important substance produced by the stomach lining is protective mucus, which prevents the stomach from digesting itself.

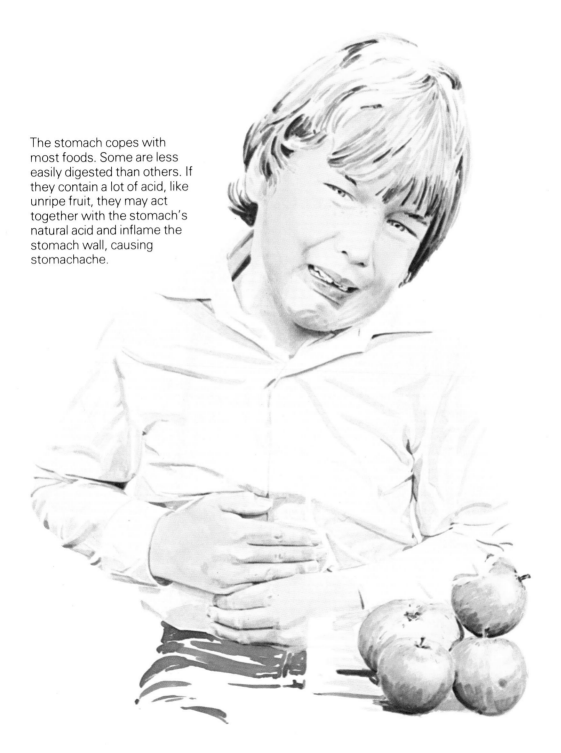

The stomach copes with most foods. Some are less easily digested than others. If they contain a lot of acid, like unripe fruit, they may act together with the stomach's natural acid and inflame the stomach wall, causing stomachache.

25

The duodenum and bile

The liquefied food that leaves the stomach is known as **chyme**. This material is thick and creamy, and passes easily into the first part of the intestine, called the duodenum. The duodenum is only about 10 in (25 cm) in length, and is bent sharply into a horseshoe shape.

The duodenum receives the strongly acid stomach contents, and it protects the rest of the intestines by neutralizing the acid chyme

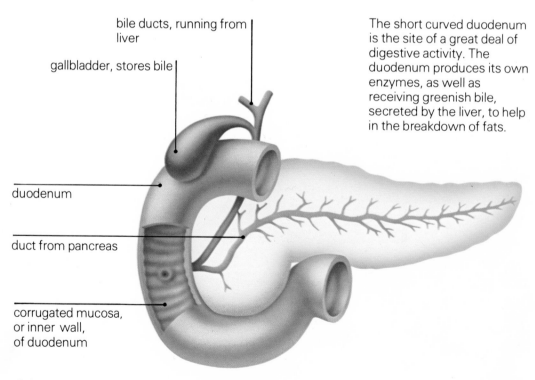

bile ducts, running from liver

gallbladder, stores bile

duodenum

duct from pancreas

corrugated mucosa, or inner wall, of duodenum

The short curved duodenum is the site of a great deal of digestive activity. The duodenum produces its own enzymes, as well as receiving greenish bile, secreted by the liver, to help in the breakdown of fats.

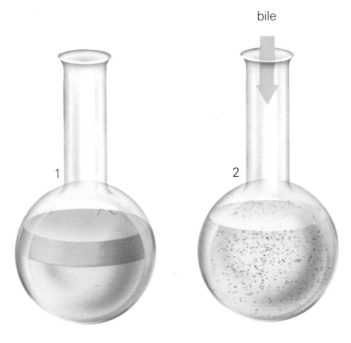

bile

Bile works like detergent on grease. It breaks up the liquid fat into globules, making a milky mixture with water called an emulsion.

1 Fats, or oils, and water do not normally mix.

2 Bile works like washing-up liquid on grease It breaks up the liquid fat into globules, making a milky mixture with water called an emulsion.

with an alkaline secretion. This also stops the action of pepsin, which only works in acid conditions. Sometimes the chyme is not neutralized enough, and attacks the gut wall, causing a duodenal ulcer (or a gastric ulcer if it happens in the stomach).

The presence of chyme and, in particular, fat in the duodenum also causes **bile** to be secreted. Bile is a greenish liquid produced in the liver and stored in the gallbladder, near the duodenum. It is released when the gallbladder contracts and is squirted through the bile duct into the duodenum. Bile contains substances which work like detergents, breaking fats into very small droplets which can be absorbed further down the intestines. Bile also contains pigments, produced by the breakdown in the liver of old red blood cells.

The pancreas

The duodenum curves around a large gland called the **pancreas**, which produces pancreatic juice. This drains into the duodenum through a tube which joins with the bile duct.

Pancreatic juice contains several important enzymes which continue the digestion of food in the chyme, making it suitable for absorption further down the intestine.

Trypsin and **chymotrypsin** are two of the enzymes which, together with several others, break down protein into amino acids. These enzymes are too powerful to be secreted in their active forms, so the pancreas produces them in inactive forms, which change in the duodenum to become enzymes.

Amylase, also in the pancreatic juice, is a starch-splitting enzyme, which continues the work begun in the mouth by ptyalin, turning starch into sugar. Lipase, another enzyme, works with the bile to break down fats into small, easily absorbed droplets.

All these reaction can only take place in the alkaline conditions of the duodenum.

Another important function of the pancreas is the production of a substance called **insulin**. This is released straight into the bloodstream, where it regulates the amount of sugar in the blood throughout the body.

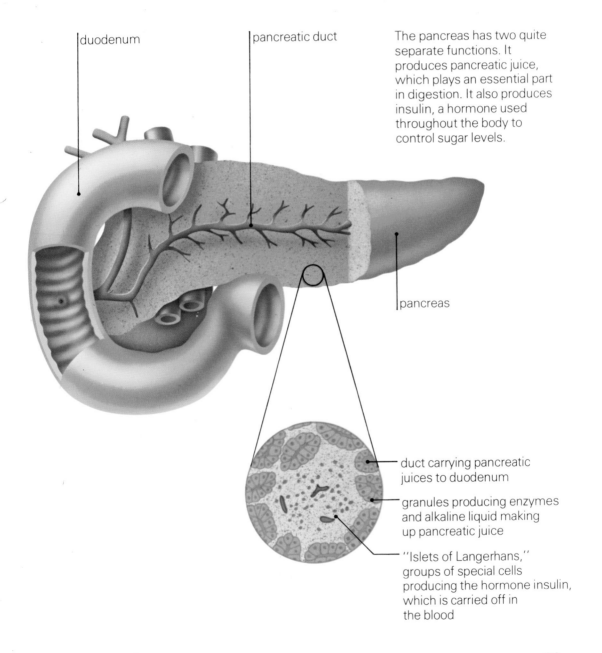

duodenum

pancreatic duct

The pancreas has two quite separate functions. It produces pancreatic juice, which plays an essential part in digestion. It also produces insulin, a hormone used throughout the body to control sugar levels.

pancreas

duct carrying pancreatic juices to duodenum

granules producing enzymes and alkaline liquid making up pancreatic juice

"Islets of Langerhans," groups of special cells producing the hormone insulin, which is carried off in the blood

29

The small intestine

The whole lining of the small intestine is covered with tiny finger-shaped villi. These give the mucosa an enormous surface area for the absorption of digested food.

1 villi

2 capillaries, carrying dissolved nutrients to the liver for storage

3 lacteals, carrying absorbed fats to the lymph system

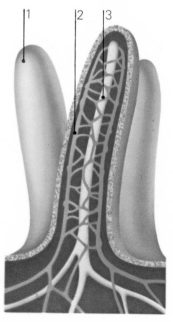

Following the duodenum is the remainder of the small intestine. It is actually very long, some 13-23 feet (4-7m) in length, but is called "small" because it is narrow.

It is divided into two further sections, called the **jejunum** and the **ileum**, but both have similar structures and functions.

Digestion is completed in the small intestine, and broken-down food materials are absorbed. The mucosa in both the duodenum and small intestine is covered with millions of tiny fingerlike projections called **villi**, which make it look like the surface of a fluffy towel. These, together with the folds in the mucosa, give the small intestine a very large surface area to help in absorbing food.

Only small amounts of enzymes are released into the small intestine. Partially digested food is absorbed into special cells covering the villi, where further breakdown continues. Here proteins complete their breakdown into amino acids, and sugars are broken down into **glucose**. These materials dissolve in the blood passing through **capillaries** in the villi, and are carried off to the liver.

Fat globules are also absorbed, and these pass into a network of fine tubes which form part of the **lymph** system.

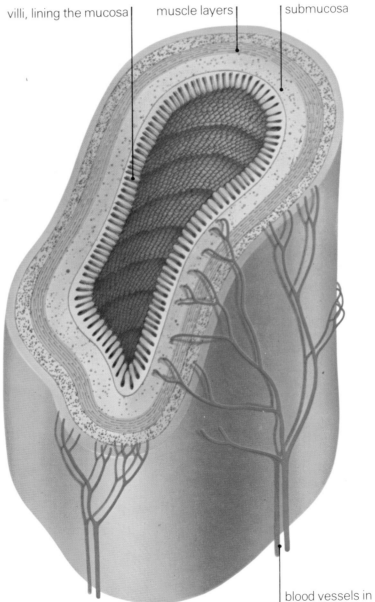

villi, lining the mucosa | muscle layers | submucosa

blood vessels in mesentery

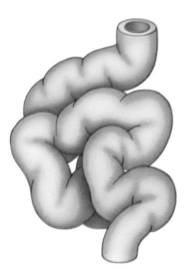

The small intestine is very long and is coiled tightly in the abdomen.

The walls of the small intestine are highly efficient in absorbing nutrients because of their very large surface area.

31

The large intestine

The joining of the small intestine to the colon marks the end of digestion. Chyme passes through a special valve into the wide colon, where it will gradually be changed from a liquid into solid feces.

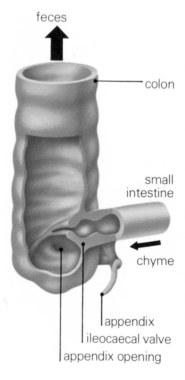

feces

colon

small intestine

chyme

appendix
ileocaecal valve
appendix opening

Water conservation is important. To prevent the body from becoming dried out, water must be reabsorbed from the liquid chyme in the small intestine. However, the remaining material is still liquid when it enters the large intestine, and here most of the water that is left is removed to produce semi-solid feces.

The large intestine is a wide tube, called the **colon**. Close to where it joins the small intestine is the **appendix**, a small projection about the size of a finger. This has no obvious function, and is thought to be a left-over from our early ancestors.

As water and salts from the chyme are reabsorbed in the colon, so the contents become steadily firmer. Mucus is secreted into the colon to lubricate the passage of this more solid material.

The final section of the large intestine is called the **rectum**. This is sensitive to the presence of feces, and as it fills, warns us that we need to defecate, or discharge feces.

Billions of harmless bacteria live in the colon, and about one-third of the weight of faeces is made up of dead bacteria. Another third is indigestible matter in the food which has passed straight through the gut. The rest is unwanted mineral salts, dead cells cast off from the gut lining, and bile.

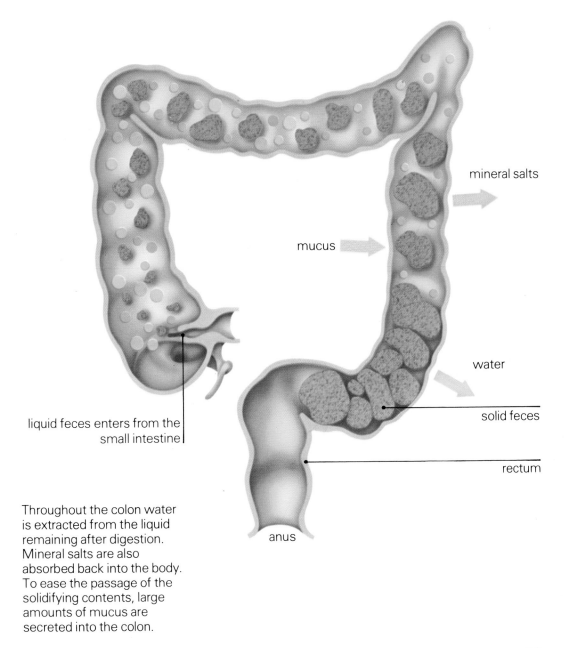

mineral salts

mucus

water

solid feces

liquid feces enters from the small intestine

rectum

anus

Throughout the colon water is extracted from the liquid remaining after digestion. Mineral salts are also absorbed back into the body. To ease the passage of the solidifying contents, large amounts of mucus are secreted into the colon.

Control of the digestive system

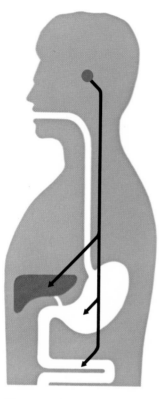

The vagus nerve is an important controller of the activity of the digestive system. The sight or thought of food causes the vagus to stimulate the stomach and intestines to begin secreting enzymes and the liver to produce bile.

The process of digestion is controlled in several different ways.

The muscle running through the gut wall contracts regularly, to give peristaltic movement, even if there is no food in the gut. These movements can be slowed down or speeded up by instructions passed from the brain along the nervous system. This regulates the speed at which food travels through the digestive system.

The sight, smell, taste or even anticipation of food causes the brain to start the digestive process working. Impulses passed from the brain start the production of saliva from the salivary glands – the mouth "waters." The peristaltic movements of the stomach increase, and acid and pepsin begin to flow in the gastric juice. This extra activity is the cause of stomach "rumbling" when we are hungry and thinking of food.

Another form of control is by chemical messengers called **hormones**. These are produced in the gut wall when it is stimulated by the presence of food. Hormones are then carried in the bloodstream to a lower part of the gut, where they trigger off another stage in the digestive process.

By the time we actually begin to eat, the anticipation has already caused the digestive system to prepare itself by producing enzymes.

Disorders of the gut

The gut is affected by many diseases and disorders. Some are caused by the corrosive liquids it contains. If the contents of the stomach leak back up the esophagus, they cause painful heartburn, so-called because the discomfort seems near the heart.

When the protective coating of the stomach or duodenum fails, or if too much acid is produced, the gastric juice eats into the gut wall, forming a pit, or ulcer.

Appendicitis is a form of inflammation caused when the appendix becomes blocked, and trapped food material decays.

Anxiety and stress can cause the brain to overstimulate the digestive system. If this continues for a long time, stress may cause ulcers due to over-production of acid. Anxiety and stress can also speed up peristalsis, and this can cause diarrhea, when food passes through the digestive system too fast for water to be reabsorbed.

If peristalsis moves too slowly, so much water is absorbed that feces become hard and are painful to pass. This condition is called constipation, and is usually relieved by eating plenty of vegetables and fruit, which contain a large amount of fiber. This "roughage" helps the passage of food through the colon, and may have other health benefits.

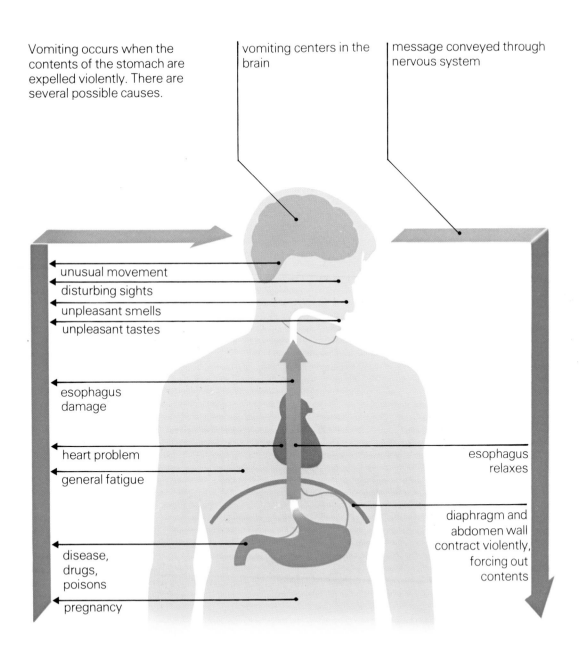

Vomiting occurs when the contents of the stomach are expelled violently. There are several possible causes.

vomiting centers in the brain

message conveyed through nervous system

unusual movement
disturbing sights
unpleasant smells
unpleasant tastes

esophagus damage

heart problem

general fatigue

disease, drugs, poisons

pregnancy

esophagus relaxes

diaphragm and abdomen wall contract violently, forcing out contents

Food transport

Blood supplies oxygen to all parts of the gut, and carries away waste materials via the tiny capillaries that penetrate the villi. There are also fine tubes in the villi called lacteals, that connect with the lymph system.

Arteries supply blood to the gut and to other other organs of the body. Veins usually return "used" blood to the heart after its oxygen has been used, but the blood leaving the gut has different uses. It contains large amounts of dissolved food materials, or **nutrients**, most of which have to be carried to the liver for temporary storage.

So this blood leaves the gut along a number of veins which join into the large **portal vein**, leading directly to the liver, instead of the heart. Other veins later carry this blood from the liver to the heart in the usual way.

Fat droplets, absorbed through the villi directly into the lacteals, pass into the lymph system and enter the main blood supply in the upper part of the chest.

All the blood vessels supplying and leaving the intestines are protected within a folded sheet of membrane called the **mesentery**. This is wrapped completely around the intestines, and supports all of the great coiled length of the system in its proper position inside the abdomen.

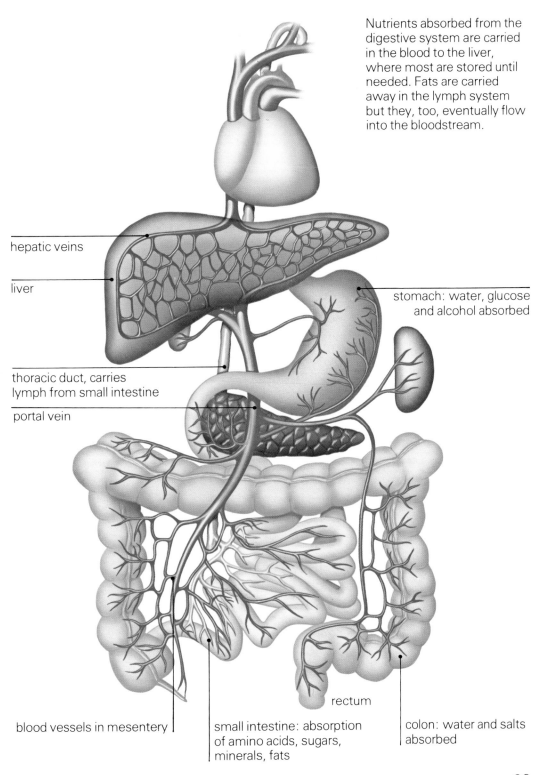

Nutrients absorbed from the digestive system are carried in the blood to the liver, where most are stored until needed. Fats are carried away in the lymph system but they, too, eventually flow into the bloodstream.

hepatic veins

liver

thoracic duct, carries lymph from small intestine

portal vein

stomach: water, glucose and alcohol absorbed

blood vessels in mesentery

small intestine: absorption of amino acids, sugars, minerals, fats

rectum

colon: water and salts absorbed

Liver function

The liver has more separate functions than any other organ of the body. So far, more than 500 different functions have been identified, and there are certainly many as yet undiscovered.

The liver receives all the nutrients absorbed from the digestive system into the blood. It processes and stores these materials and also manufactures a wide range of essential substances.

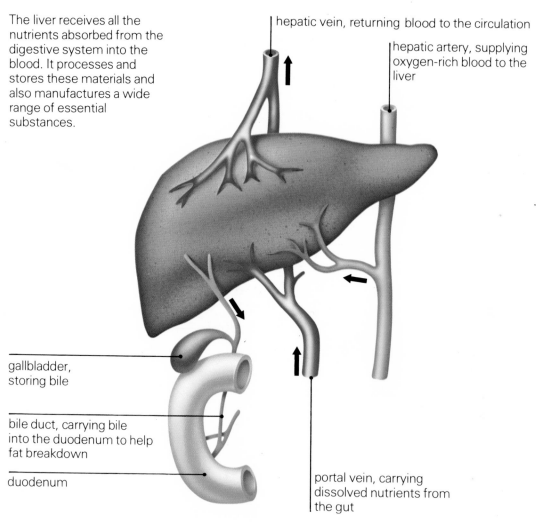

hepatic vein, returning blood to the circulation

hepatic artery, supplying oxygen-rich blood to the liver

gallbladder, storing bile

bile duct, carrying bile into the duodenum to help fat breakdown

duodenum

portal vein, carrying dissolved nutrients from the gut

When nutrients reach the liver in the blood supply from the gut, some are broken down still further. Many amino acids are split in the liver, producing energy-giving materials, as well as urea, a waste product which passes out in the urine.

Amino acids are also built up again into proteins in the liver, and these are carried off in the blood for use around the body. Substances which help blood to clot are also produced here.

Glucose is converted to a substance called **glycogen**, which is stored in the liver until needed. Glycogen can be broken down very fast to provide quick bursts of energy. Fats are also stored in the liver, but are broken down more slowly to provide energy.

Red blood cells have only a short life, and are broken down in the liver to produce bile. Red blood cells contain iron, and this material is stored in the liver for future use.

Another very important function of the liver is to deal with poisonous substances such as alcohol and drugs, which enter the bloodstream, and to make them harmless.

Liver structure

The liver is the largest gland in the body, weighing about $4\frac{1}{2}$ lb (2 kg). It lies mainly on the right of the body, level with the stomach. The liver is flat in shape and soft in texture, with a very large blood supply.

The whole liver, with its huge range of functions, is built up from simple units called lobules. These are flat sheets of liver cells, arranged so that they fan out from a central vein. Between these sheets of cells are large spaces through which blood flows, bathing each cell. Each lobule is six-sided, and about 1/8 in (3 mm) across. The hexagonal shape of a lobule can easily be seen in a piece of fresh animal liver.

Blood coming into the liver from the portal vein, carrying nutrients from the gut, flows through the spaces in the lobules. It brings materials to be stored or processed, and carries away substances produced by the tiny liver cells.

Packed inside the sheets of liver cells is a network of fine tubes into which bile is secreted. These connect and enlarge to form the bile duct.

All the liver's functions are carried out by the same types of liver cell, which are present in huge numbers.

liver lobules | vein, leading to hepatic vein

bile caniculi, tubes carrying bile to the bile duct

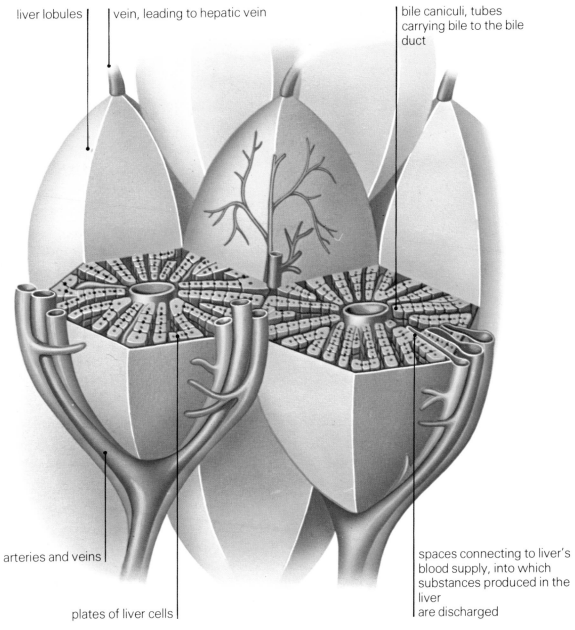

arteries and veins

plates of liver cells

spaces connecting to liver's blood supply, into which substances produced in the liver are discharged

43

Overeating and malnutrition

Most of the food we eat is used to produce energy. A small part is needed for growth, and replacement of damaged tissue. We need proportionately more food during childhood and adolescence than we do as adults, when growth has stopped.

In the developed nations of the world, where food is plentiful, most people are overweight, due to eating more food than is needed for body repair or energy supply. Instead, the extra food material is stored as fat, but because we are not very active, the fat store is not used, and we become overweight, which can cause health problems. To lose this weight, we must eat less or exercise more – preferably both together.

For nearly half of the world's population, food shortage is a problem. Cereals can usually be grown, giving a good supply of carbohydrates which, when digested to form sugars, provide an adequate supply of energy. But protein shortage is a more serious problem. In the poorer nations of the world it is usually too expensive or difficult to raise livestock for meat. Protein deficiency has serious effects on growing children and may cause permanent damage in later life. A poorly balanced diet may also lack the vitamins and minerals needed for health.

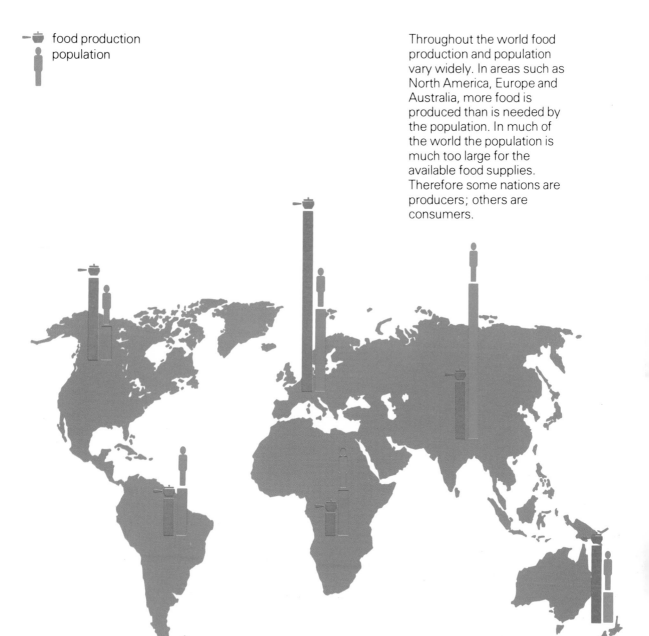

food production
population

Throughout the world food
production and population
vary widely. In areas such as
North America, Europe and
Australia, more food is
produced than is needed by
the population. In much of
the world the population is
much too large for the
available food supplies.
Therefore some nations are
producers; others are
consumers.

Glossary

Alkali: a substance that can neutralize an acid, making it inactive. There are alkaline conditions in the duodenum which neutralize stomach acid.

Amino acids: the basic building blocks which make up proteins. Foods containing protein are broken down into their amino acids during digestion.

Amylase: an enzyme present in the pancreatic juice. It completes the digestion of starch into sugar, which can then be absorbed.

Anus: the opening at the end of the digestive system through which feces are discharged.

Appendix: a finger-sized projection at the top of the colon. Sometimes it becomes inflamed, causing appendicitis.

Bile: a greenish liquid produced in the liver and stored in the gallbladder. It is passed into the duodenum to help in the breakdown of fat into small globules which can be absorbed.

Capillaries: tiny blood vessels penetrating every organ of the body, and connecting arteries to veins. Capillary walls are very thin, so small food molecules can pass through them and enter the bloodstream.

Carbohydrate: a food substance that provides energy. Sugars and starches are carbohydrates. Bread is a rich source.

Cellulose: material making up the cell walls of plants. Cellulose is indigestible, and passes through the digestive system unchanged.

Chyme: the semi-liquid contents of the gut after it leaves the stomach. It comprises partly digested food material, digestive juices and mucus.

Chymotrypsin: an enzyme found in pancreatic juice which digests protein.

Colon: the large intestine. Wide part of the gut in which water and mineral salts are reabsorbed from digested food remains to produce solid feces.

Duodenum: the short section of the small intestine leading from the stomach. The pancreas and bile duct pour their secretions into the duodenum.

Enzyme: a substance which causes the breakdown or digestion of food material. Enzymes remain unchanged during this process.

Esophagus: the gullet; the section of gut carrying food from the mouth to the stomach.

Fat: a greasy substance, which may be a solid or an oil. Fat is an energy source and is stored in the body.

Feces: solid waste material remaining after digestion. Consists principally of indigestible material and the remains of bacteria living in the gut.

Fiber: indigestible plant material, forming an important part of the diet. Fiber adds bulk to the feces, preventing constipation as well as disorders of the lower gut.

Fundus: the broad upper part of the stomach, where food is stored temporarily.

Glucose: a form of sugar which can be broken down to release energy.

Glycogen: the form in which carbohydrate is stored in the body. It can be rapidly broken down into glucose when energy is needed.

Gut: the long tube extending from mouth to anus, making up the digestive system.

Hormone: a chemical messenger produced by a gland and released into the blood, which carries it so that the hormone can provide instructions to another part of the body.

Hydrochloric acid: the strong acid secreted into the stomach, where it provides proper conditions to start the digestion of protein. Hydrocholoric acid is neutralized by the alkaline conditions in the duodenum.

Ileum: the lower part of the small intestine.

Insulin: a substance produced in the pancreas and released directly into the blood. It regulates the amount of sugar in the blood, and its absence causes diabetes.

Intestine: the length of gut between the stomach and anus, comprising small intestine, colon and rectum.

Jejunum: the middle section of the small intestine.

Lymph: a milky liquid circulated in the lymph system. Lymph resembles blood from which all the red cells have been filtered. Lymph carries fat absorbed from the intestines.

Mesentery: thin sheet of tissue, with many blood vessels, which supports the gut in the abdomen, supplies it with blood, and carries digested nutrients away in the bloodstream to the liver.

Minerals: substances used in building bones, teeth and many other parts of the body. Minerals are not digested, but are absorbed unchanged from food in the gut.

Mucosa: the inner lining of the gut, containing glands.

Mucus: a slippery, watery material produced from the mucosa. It protects the gut and lubricates solid waste passing through the colon and rectum.

Nutrient: a food substance, in a form capable of being used by the body.

Oxygen: a colorless gas, present in the air, needed by all the cells of the body.

Pancreas: a gland which secretes a mixture of enzymes into the duodenum. Also secretes insulin into the blood.

Pepsin: an enzyme produced in the stomach, which begins the digestion of protein.

Pepsinogen: a substance released from the stomach wall and changed into the enzyme pepsin by the action of hydrochloric acid.

Peristalsis: the wavelike muscular movement of the walls of the whole digestive system, which carries food along.

Portal vein: the blood vessel which carries absorbed nutrients from the gut to the liver.

Protein: food substances derived from meat and from some vegetables, nuts and cereals. Important in building muscle.

Ptyalin: an enzyme in the saliva which starts the breakdown of starch into sugar.

Pylorus: the lower part of the stomach, in which food is mixed and churned, and digestion of protein begins.

Rectum: the lowest part of the large intestine. Short length of gut in which feces are temporarily stored before discharge through the anus.

Sphincter: a ring of muscle, acting as a valve to control the flow of material through the gut.

Starch: a form of carbohydrate derived from plant materials. Must be turned into sugar through digestion before it can be used by the body.

Submucosa: the middle layer of the gut wall, between the mucosa and muscle layers.

Sugars: mostly sweet-tasting carbohydrates. Mostly obtained from plant materials, and used in the body to supply energy.

Trypsin: a protein-digesting enzyme in pancreatic juice.

Villi: tiny fingerlike projections covering the lining of the small intestine through which nutrients are absorbed. Villi increase the area of the gut lining, making food absorption more efficient.

Vitamins: food substances, usually present in very tiny quantities, which are essential for good health.

Index